MUSEO DEL PRADO

GUIDE

Quick visit

Alicia Quintana

ALDEASA

The main Hall in «El Comercio»

THE MUSEUM

The Prado Museum is a neo-Classical building by the Architect Juan de
Villanueva, the construction of which began in the year 1785. It
was conceived of as a museum and natural history room forming
part of a building complex dedicated to the study of science, as
planned under the reign of Charles III and within the scope of
the urban reform that took place on the Paseo del Prado
(previously named Salón del Prado), which was also embellished
with various monumental fountains (Cybele, Apollo and
Neptune).

It was established in 1819 as the «Royal Museum of Painting and
Sculpture» by King Ferdinand VII, with pieces from the royal
collections amassed by earlier Spanish Monarchs, his forebears.
At the end of the 19th century, the Museum —by then national
in scope— received works from another museum, then called the
Trinity, that were of a eclesiastic nature and which had been
expropriated under laws governing the depreciation of
ecclesiastic assets. From the time of the creation and merger of
the two museums many other works of art have been added to
the Prado through donations, legacies and acquisitions.

Brambila. The Prado Museum, around 1840

Brambila. North Rotunda of the Prado Museum, around 1830

Only a tenth of the museum's artistic holdings are actually on display in its two buildings, the Villanueva Building and the Casón del Buen Retiro. The remainder is held in other places, museums, institutions and Government buildings or in storage at specially conditioned sites within the two museum buildings.

The large museum collections fundamentally include paintings. However, there is a valuable collection of sculptures, drawings, furniture, luxury art, coins and medallions that cannot be permanently displayed due to lack of space.

The Painting collection (12th to the 20th century) is displayed as followed: up to the 18th century and Goya's work is in the Villanueva Building, and the 19th and 20th centuries' work in the nearby Casón del Buen Retiro.

The fundamental painting collections belong to the Spanish schools —the best represented— and the Italian and Flemish schools. The French, Dutch and German schools, though numerically less represented, are not unworthy of mention vis-à-vis their quality. Two halls are expressly reserved for sculpture, but sculptural pieces are scattered throughout the different halls in both museum buildings. All decorative art is on display in what is known as the Dauphin's Treasure.

The tour we propose will allow you to view the fifty most famous pieces of the museum. The normal placement of these pieces are indicated, though it is possible (due to remodeling or temporary expositions) these may be found to have been altered. If this is the case, the museum guards will provide further information.

VELÁZQUEZ. «Las Meninas» (detail)

VILLANUEVA BUILDING

This building offers the museum's painting collection from the 12th century up to Goya. Regarding sculpture, on display are Greco-Roman pieces up to the 18th-century.

The Dauphin's Treasure is on display in the «Planta Sótano», or lower level.

The paintings exhibited on the museum's street level are from the Spanish schools, from the 12th to the 16th centuries (and also the Black Paintings by Goya), and the Flemish, German and Dutch schools.

On the Main Floor you will find the rest of the paintings in question — from El Greco to Goya— that make up the Spanish, Italian and French school collections. There are also several sculptures on display in the various halls.

*The tour of the fundamental pieces we propose begins on this level,
after entering by way of the North Door (Lower Door or Goya Door).*

MASTER OF MADERUELO (anonymous)

1 **Mural Paintings from the Holy Cross Hermitage in Maderuelo** (Segovia)
   (Cat. 7269 a 7287)

   Chapel (498 × 450 cm) transferred to canvas and reinstalled
   Spanish school. Romanesque
   12th century
   Hall 51c

The mural paintings that decorated the Chapel of the Holy Cross, in the
Segovian town of Maderuelo, were transferred to canvas in 1947 and
installed in the Prado Museum where their original setting was
recreated. The Chapel is a space measuring just over twenty square
metres and covered with a half barrel vault. The paintings that decorate
it are frescoes, though the paint is now on canvas. On the two small
walls they show apostles, angels and evangelical scenes, while at the
front of the Chapel are two biblical scenes: The Creation of Adam and
the Original Sin at the base; and the Offering of Cain and Abel to the
Mystic Lamb at the head. On the vault is the characteristic
representation of Christ as the Almighty («Pantocrator»), seated on a
throne and bestowing a blessing. The figures that are represented are
typically Romanesque in that they show neither volume nor depth, nor
do they appear to occupy a place in space: only certain surroundings
that are strongly set apart by the artist —whose style is closely related to
the Master of Tahull —allow him to brusquely separate the figures from
the neutral background.

1

BARTOLOMÉ BERMEJO (worked between 1474 and 1495)

2 St. Dominic of Silos Enthroned as Abbot (Cat. 1323)

Wood (242 × 130 cm)
Spanish school. Hispano-Flemish Gothic
15th century
Hall 49

This is one of the most monumental of all Spanish paintings from the Middle Ages; and not only due to its size, which was not common in the Spanish art of that period, but because of the remarkable excellence of the saint in question. This is the monk Dominic who founded the Silos Monastery (Burgos) in the 11th century and was its first abbot. The artist, an Andalusian painter who worked mostly in the kingdom of Aragón, shows the saint as a bishop, dressed in the characteristic trappings of such a position —pluvial cape, mitre and staff— and seated on a throne whose composition is practically architectural in scope. In its niches are representations of the Christian virtues: three theological, four cardinal. Of note is the realism of the saint's face (Flemish influence) over an abundance of gold-leaf (a genuinely Spanish tradition).

ROGER VAN DER WEYDEN (1400-1464)

3 The Deposition From the Cross (Cat. 2825)

Wood (222 × 262 cm)
Flemish school. Gothic
15th century
Hall 58

This panel was painted by Weyden for a church in Lovain (Belgium). It was later acquired by Queen Mary of Hungary, from whom it was then inherited by her nephew, Philip II, the King of Spain. In it, the meticulous study of the composition of a large group of figures placed in a very small space merits attention. The organisation of the whole appears enclosed as if by two parentheses — to the left is St. John, to the right, Mary Magdalen — with the cross serving as a kind of axis, while the focal point of the composition is formed by two parallel figures, Christ and Mary, arranged diagonally. The feeling of drama, of contained sadness, in the faces of the figures confirms Weyden as one of the most tragic of the so-called «primitive» painters of the Flemish school (15th c.).

2

3

HIERONYMUS VAN AEKEN BOSCH,
« EL BOSCO » (1450-1516)

4 The Table of the Seven Deadly Sins (Cat 2822)

Wood (120 × 150 cm)
(1450-1516)
Flemish school. Gothic
15th century
Hall 57a

This work belonged to Philip II and, as was the case with all the Bosch works
the king enjoyed collecting, it was kept at El Escorial. From there it was
transferred to the Prado during the Spanish Civil War along with other
paintings whose safety was thought to be in jeopardy given the nature of
the fighting in the mountains north of Madrid. Following the war, it simply
remained at the Prado. It consists of four small circles surrounding a larger
one that is divided into different scenes. In the corners Bosch depicts the
four stages of man: Death, Judgement, Hell and Heaven. The central circle
forms a large eye in whose centre appears the figure of the risen Christ and
the Latin inscription «Cave, cave, dominus videt» (Beware, beware, God sees
you). Around the small circle, which might be described as the eye's pupil,
are scenes alluding to the seven capital sins: Anger, Pride, Lust, Sloth,
Gluttony, Avarice and Envy. Each one shows a scene from daily life in the
Netherlands at that time. Without a doubt Bosch, a great observer and moral
critic, was especially gifted when it came to depicting the daily life of
his age.

HIERONYMUS VAN AEKEN BOSCH,
« EL BOSCO » (1450-1516)

5 The Garden of Delights (or «The Madroño Painting») (Cat.2823)

Wooden Triptych (206 × 386 cm)
Flemish school. Gothic
15th-16th centuries
Hall 57a

This painting is the most famous, most studied and also the most enigmatic
and difficult to analyse of all those done by Bosch. On the left is the
Creation of Man; in the centre are the worldly pleasures and sins; and Hell
with its punishments for all those sins on the right. Some art historians
believe that Bosch may have painted this work as an illustration of the beliefs
of a heretical sect, called the Adamites — after the nakeness of Adam —
which defended nudism and free sexual relations. In general, however, it is
believed that, as is the case throughout Bosch's work, that it is a moral satire
on the destiny of human nature, with a great quantity of symbols that still
have not been satisfactorily interpreted.

4

5

ANTHONIS VAN DASHORST MOR,
«ANTONIO MORO» (1519-1567)

6 Queen Mary of England, Second Wife of Philip II (Cat. 2108)

Wood (109 × 84 cm)
Flemish school. Renaissance
16th century
Hall 56

Antonio Moro —known as such in Spain where he worked at the courts of Charles V and Philip II— is one of the finest portrait artists in the history of painting. And this work, one his best, confirms him as a creator of a type of court protrait that would establish a school for this genre, the influence of which would reach as far as Velázquez. The lady represented was Mary Tudor, and in her right hand is the pink rose of this dynasty. With such an arrogant gesture and distant gaze, together with the severe countenance that has passed its prime, Moor was able to reflect in a majestic way the effect of a life full of suffering and sadness. Mary Tudor was known as Bloody Mary due to the fierceness employed to reestablish the Catholicism that her father, Henry VIII, had abolished. Besides Philip II's second wife, she was also his aunt.

PIETER BRUEGEL «THE ELDER» (1525/30-1569)

7 The Triumph of Death (Cat. 1393)

Wood (117 × 162 cm)
Flemish school. Renaissance
16th century
Hall 56a

Bruegel, the Elder, the patriarch of a long dynasty of like-named painters, was a characteristically Flemish painter of the Renaissance Period. Though he knew the Italian Renaissance and had even travelled to Italy, he preferred to conserve the essences and traditions of the so-called «primitives» and the spirit of the popular, critical, satirical and moralistic inspiration of Bosch. In this work, quite complex given the quantity of scenes, he wished to represent the triumph of Death over all earthly things —as in the Danses Macabres of medieval literature. The version he gives us is that of an anguished end without the least bit of hope: even the sombre colours of the bare earth and of the background fires accentuate Man's uneasiness before Death's arrival. Death rides in on a squalid horse, with a scythe, pushing humanity against an army of skeletons shielded with coffin lids.

6

7

ALBRECHT DÜRER, «DURERO» (1471-1528)

8   Self-portrait (Cat. 2179)

Wood (52×41 cm)
German school. Renaissance.
15th century
Hall 54

Albrecht Dürer, the son of a Hungarian goldsmith who had taken up
residence in Nüremberg, was the leading Renaissance figure of northern
Europe. He travelled twice to Italy and was able to assimilate there the
trends of the age's new style. Nevertheless, he never forgot the German
Gothic tradition of great strength and meticulous interest in drawing.
This self-portrait is one of three that have been preserved, and in it he
depicts himself at the age of 23; this is confirmed in the inscription,
which together with his characteristic signature can be found just
beneath the line of the window. He appears from the waist up wearing
elegant, low-cut attire that gives him a certain Italian air, in the style of
a noble gentleman; painters had never before been represented with
this kind of graceful bearing in the Middle Ages.

PETER PAUL RUBENS (1577-1640)

9   The Adoration of the Magi (Cat 1638)

Canvas (346×488 cm)
Flemish school. Baroque
17th century
Hall 61b

This painting is one of the largest at the Prado. Originally smaller in size,
Rubens himself enlarged it —adding on to the top and the right side—
twenty years after he first painted it. He had done it for the Government
of his city, Antwerp; by way of the Spanish governor, it reached Philip IV,
who contracted Rubens to enlarge it during the painter's second stay at
Madrid's royal court. Part of the addition on the right is Ruben's own
self-portrait — he is the horseman in purple craning his neck to look at
the spectator. It is one of his most spectacular and unrestrained works,
albeit organised around a diagonal axis which acts as a kind of vertebra
of the composition, that runs from the figure of the Child, to the
opposite corner.

8

9

PETER PAUL RUBENS (1577-1640)

10   The Three Graces (Cat. 1670)

Wood (221 × 181 cm)
Flemish school. Baroque
17th century
Hall 61

This work, painted late in the artist's career, remained in Ruben's
personal collection until it was auctioned, along with other personal
items, upon his death, when it was acquired by a representative of Philip
IV. For a good part of the 18th century this painting was stored, along
with other nudes —considered sinful by Charles III — in a secret gallery
at the Academy of Fine Arts. The Graces were Zeus' three daughters,
considered in mythology to be the goddesses of revelry and joy in the
service of Aphrodite, the goddess of love. The Grace on the left is
actually a portrait of the artist's second wife, a girl Rubens wed when he
was nearing sixty and she was sixteen. Rubens often resorted to using
Helen Fourment's opulently curvaceous figure as a model for female
images.

10

ANTON VAN DYCK (1599-1641)

11 Sir Endymion Porter and Van Dyck (Cat. 1489)

Canvas (119 x 144 cm)
Flemish school. Baroque
17th century
Hall 62b

This double portrait —a genre not commonly found in the history of painting— shows the artist, Anton Van Dyck, and his friend, the English aristocrat and collector, Sir Endymion Porter. Van Dyck, who left his native Flanders upon accepting a contract offered him by Charles I, the King of England, would complete the bulk of his work in England; there he established contacts with members of British high society —given his post as Court Painter— and he would profoundly influence later English painting. Besides being a double portrait, the artist also contrasted several «dualities»: the white garb of his friend compares to the artist's dark cloak; the background framing Porter is an open space, while Van Dyck is seen in an interior setting; the very shape of the painting is oval, a figure obtained by cutting two circles secantly, which hides a reflection of this juxtapositioning, since each portrait would be contained in one of the respective imaginary circles even the delicate, bare hand of the artist contrasts to the dark, gloved hand of the Englishman. Art historians concur in the opinion that this portrait is one of the most elegant of the Baroque period.

11

REMBRANDT HARMENSZ VAN RIJN (1606-1669)

12 Artemisia (Cat. 2132)

Canvas (142 × 153 cm)
Dutch school. Baroque
17th century
Hall 59

This is the only Rembrandt owned by the Prado Museum; it came to form part of the Spanish royal collections when Charles III acquired it in the 18th century, along with other personal possessions of the Marquis de la Ensenada, upon the nobleman's death. The woman, dressed in a yellowish white gown with embroidered sleeves and ermine about the shoulders, appears to be receiving a goblet. If one accepts the premise that this is Queen Artemisia (there are other possible interpretations), the goblet would contain the ashes of her husband, King Mausolus, which the widow was to drink. Another opinion has it that the painting is a depiction of Queen Sophonisba, who had to drink the poison sent to her by her husband so as to avoid falling into the hands of their enemies. Whatever the case, this could be a symbolic representation of marital fidelity, since Rembrandt painted it in the same year he was married (1634).

FRANCISCO DE GOYA Y LUCIENTES (1746-1828)

13 Saturn Devouring One of his Sons (Cat. 763)

Mural transfered to canvas (146 × 83 cm)
Spanish school
19th century
Hall 66

This disconcerting painting is one of the fourteen known as the «black paintings» with which Goya decorated the dining and sitting rooms of his home, called the «Quinta del Sordo», which he bought in 1819 on the banks of Madrid's Manzanares River. Seventy years after they were painted, the owner decided to have them taken down and put on canvas given their deteriorated condition. Some years later he would donate them to the Spanish state. Saturn Devouring One of his Sons was one of the six works decorating the dining room. It depicts a scene from mythology —the god Saturn, or Cronus— that acts as an allegorical illusion to the artist's own day. The god devoured Cybele and his children, as time devours all that it creates: he feared that one would rise up and destroy him.

12

13

14 Onyx Saltcellar With Gold Mermaid

(N° 1 in The Dauphin's Treasure)
17 cms. in height
16th century
Hall 101 (Lower Level)

This is the most representative of the hard-stone pieces included in the
Dauphin's Treasure; there are other pieces worked in rock crystal. The
Dauphin's Treasure is a collection of rich decorative pieces that once
belonged to the heir to the French throne under Louis XIV, known as the
Dauphin. Part of the inheritance of this great collector (who died before
his father and thus never became king) was passed to his son,
Philip d'Anjou, who had assumed the throne of Spain twelve years
earlier and was known as Philip V of Bourbon. The collection includes
goblets, cups and trays with glasses of all types and beautiful pouring
vessels. The saltcellar is a very original piece in which the mermaid is an
allusion to the marine origin of salt. The figure is made of gold, with
enamel-covered legs and body adorned with magnificent rubies, nearly
two hundred in all. The vessel is made out of brown, white-striped
agate.

14

To continue the Masterpieces Tour, one must procede now to the Main Floor of the Villanueva Building. To do so, return to the Ground Floor and take the stairs across the lobby at the South, or Murillo, Door.

FRANCISCO DE GOYA Y LUCIENTES (1746-1828)

15 The Wine Harvest (Cat. 795)

Canvas (275 × 190 cm)
Spanish school
18th century
Hall 23

Goya began his artistic activity in Madrid as a tapestry cartoon painter at the Santa Barbara Royal Tapestry Factory, which produced decorative tapestries for the different royal sites. This cartoon was painted by Goya for the King's Dining Room (Charles III) at the El Pardo Palace (Madrid). Goya created it as part of series dedicated to the seasons of the year. The wine harvest represents autumn, and the three other tapestries, symbolising the remaining seasons, also hung in the same room. This is a very serene composition, with the figures in the foreground grouped as if within a squat triangle. The colouring is very pure, and the fields of colour are clearly set apart: this was to facilitate the work of the tapestry weavers. The basket propped atop the head of one of the figures is considered one of the finest Spanish still lifes.

15

FRANCISCO DE GOYA Y LUCIENTES
(1746-1828)

16   The 3rd of May 1808 in Madrid: the Executions on Príncipe Pío Hill (Cat. 749)

Canvas (268 × 347 cm)
Spanish school
19th century
Hall 39

This emblematic work —and its counterpart, the 2nd of May, which is on
display in the same hall— were painted by Goya in 1814 when he was
commissioned by the Regency Council governing Spain following the
War of Independence. The paintings were to «perpetuate the most
notable and heroic feats of our glorious insurrection against the tyrant
of Europe» and were hung on the Arch of Triumph that was built to
honour the return to Madrid of King Ferdinand VII. The event depicted
in this work is the violent French repression of the patriots who rose up
in rebellion on 2 May, 1808 against the invading forces of Napoleon.
This painting has been considered the greatest symbol of independence
and of the defence of liberty of the Spanish people. However, it has also
doubtlessly become a universal statement about war and its
consequences. With the force of the tragedy so readily depicted, Goya
became the most important forebear of the contemporary artistic
movement known as Expressionism.

16

FRANCISCO DE GOYA Y LUCIENTES (1746-1828)

17 The Clothed Maja (Cat. 741)
The Nude Maja (Cat.742)

Canvas (95 × 188 cm)
Canvas (98 × 191 cm)
Spanish school
19th century
Hall 36

The word «maja» used to describe the women in these two paintings is actually a recent title, despite the fact that the term certainly existed in the 18th century; it referred to women of the lower social class in Madrid who were characterised by a certain freedom of customs and an extroverted pertness. However, the titles of these paintings as recorded in the inventory of the personal effects of Charles IV's Minister, Manuel Godoy, their first owner, used the word «Gitana», or Gypsy. It is logical to suppose that the paintings were part of a kind of mischievous game of that day and age whereby the clothed figure was placed over the nude. It is interesting to note how the garb of the Clothed Maja is tucked in such a way as to make her seem even more «nude» than her unclad counterpart.

What is certain is that the technique employed by Goya also accentuates this sensual aspect: the brush strokes with which the Clothed Maja is painted —loose, soft, very free —contrast with the polished academic perfection of the Nude Maja. In both cases the woman's head, showing a plain face wearing a bit of a smirk, is of scant importance vis-à-vis the beauty of the bodies.

17

FRANCISCO DE GOYA Y LUCIENTES (1746-1828)

18 Charles IV and his Family (Cat. 720)

Canvas (280 × 336 cm)
Spanish school
19th century
Hall 32

Goya did this collective portrait of the family of Charles IV, who had named him to the post of Court Painter, in the year 1800; in fact it was the last royal portrait he would paint. Once more we can see that, while other painters represented the monarchs «as they should be», Goya rendered them «as they really were.» And in this large canvas he did not hold back his lack of affection for an expired monarch of such scant effect, much like the one the French revolutionaries had dethroned to the north. Goya subscribed to the ideas of the Enlightenment and was accused of being «Frenchified». The Royal Family seems to be presided over by Queen Maria Luisa, as was the case in fact, instead of by the king. Goya included himself, by way of a self-portrait, before a canvas on the left of the painting, as Velázquez had done many years before when he paintied the Family of Philip IV, called Las Meninas. Goya always recognised Velázquez, together with Rembrandt and Mother Nature, as his only three teachers. His technique, loose brush strokes that seem almost impressionistic, reached one of its highest levels in this painting.

18

BARTOLOMÉ ESTEBAN MURILLO (1618-1682)

19 The Immaculate Conception of Soult (Cat. 2809)

Canvas (274 × 190 cm)
Spanish school. Baroque
17th century
Hall 16b

Murillo, in line with his taste for religious topics and devotion, consecrated for the posterity of art history the representation of the Virgin as the Immaculate Conception. The so-called «de Soult» is doubtlessly one of the most beautiful and famous of all those he painted. Its name comes from the French marshall who stole it during the War of Independence from the chapel of Seville's Venerables Hospital, for which it was commissioned. It was not returned to Spain until 1940; it was kept at the Louvre for almost the entirety of its absence. In these representations by Murillo, in which he consecrated the popular devotion to Mary's «spotless» conception, the Virgin is generally a young woman of great beauty wearing a white tunic and blue cloak and surrounded by angels and clouds. She also rests her feet on a pedestal of clouds while stepping on a serpent, or half-moon, the symbol of Lucifer when he tricked Eve into committing the original sin in Eden. That was when God the Father warned the devil that: «a woman will crush your head.»

BARTOLOMÉ ESTEBAN MURILLO (1618-1682)

20 The Good Shepherd (Cat. 962)

Canvas (123 × 101 cm)
Spanish shcool. Baroque
17th century
Hall 16b

In this Murillo canvas the soft, vapourous style that made him famous stands out more than ever. Murillo often showed the saints as children, thus accentuating the devoutness of the faithful through the use of such tender symbols. In this particular case, the paintings shows a young Jesus as the good shepherd, representing him in fact as Christ described himself, since in public he would say he was «the good shepherd who gives his life for his sheep.» Thus, the Child holds a shepherd's staff in his right hand and rests the left on the back of a sheep, rendered with prodigious naturalism by Murillo. The canvas, originally smaller, was added on to —the addition is evident— by Murillo himself when a painting of the same theme was needed for a later decoration project.

19

20

FRANCISCO DE ZURBARÁN (1598-1664)

21 Still Life (Cat. 2803)

Canvas (46 x 84 cm)
Spanish school. Baroque
17th century
Hall 17a

Still lifes, of course, are those paintings that reveal the essence of every day objects in a kind of immediate reality. However, these works of apparently slight intrinsic importance are treated by the artist with the attention and interest that is more often associated with the great artistic themes. It was a genre that was especially beloved in the Baroque Period, since it was by means of such work that the realism characterising the age was truly created. Zurbarán gives us absolute simplicity in his still life along with a most stunning sense of veracity. The organisation and placement of the objects could hardly be less complicated: a bronze cup on a silver tray, a white clay vessel, another in red and a small white jug on a silver tray, all simply arranged on a board. One's impression is that it is real —because also real are the quantities of the items represented— items that belong to a neat, orderly, serene world.

JOSÉ DE RIBERA (1591-1662)

22 The Martyrdom of St. Philip (Cat. 1101)

Canvas (234 x 234 cm)
Spanish and Italian schools. Baroque
17th century
Hall 16a

José de Ribera, born in Xátiva (Valencia), practiced his profession in Italy, mainly in Naples, where he was known as «lo Spagnoletto». This is the reason he is considered to belong to the Italian school. Setting him apart from his Spanish contemporary was his special love of colour and the classical air of his figures and compositions. His interest in colour came from his knowledge of Venetian painting; and the classical world is present —as it is in this painting— in the evocation of Roman ruins. In this painting, often considered to be a paradigm of the Baroque naturalists, Ribera presents the preparation of the Apostle-Martyr Philip, who was submitted to the torment of being skinned alive. A tenebrist and realist, Ribera shows his great compositional skills through the treatment of light with which he presents the nudity of the saint — with a predominent diagonal line that organises the scene. We also see his skills of conveying movement and of rendering the force of the gestures of the executioners who lift the saint's body.

21

22

DIEGO VELÁZQUEZ DE SILVA (1599-1660)

23 The Surrender of Breda or The Lances (Cat. 1172)

Canvas (307 x 367 cm)
Spanish school. Baroque
17th century
Hall 16

This was one of the paintings of war scenes or Spanish military victories that decorated the so-called Kingdoms Hall at Madrid's Buen Retiro Palace. Since the palace was built for Philip IV, Velázquez, who was his artistic advisor and Court Painter, was placed in charge of decorating it. He decided to represent the victory of Spanish arms in the paintings he would do for the lateral walls of the large hall. Portraits on horseback of the king's parents, the king himself, his wife and his heir would preside over the hall at the front end. All of these paintings are now at the Prado. The commemorative canvases of the different victories were commissioned to different painters. Velázquez reserved the celebration of the rendition of the Dutch city of Breda in 1625 for himself (Holland would gain independence from Spain 15 years later). The painting is a marvel of sage composition, with the group of victors and and the group of vanquished separate and reined in by the figure of a horse; the groups form a kind of parentheses that frames the scene, which is centered on the embrace between the Spaniard, Ambrosio de Spinola, and Justine of Nassau for the Dutch.

23

DIEGO VELÁZQUEZ DE SILVA (1599-1660)

24 The Triumph of Bacchus, or «The Drunkards» (Cat. 1170)

Canvas (165 × 225 cm)
Spanish school. Baroque
17th century
Hall 15a

Velázquez, one of the few Spanish painters to depict mythological scenes, has been often accused of treating the feats and tales of the classical gods with little respect and even of making fun of them. Actually, however, guided by his magnificent realism he simply brought the gods down to the mortal world. The best and most realistic way to present the triumph of the god of wine — Bacchus for the Romans and Dionysius for the Greeks — was to show him among a group of drunkards, a common, every day scene of the age. Velázquez painted it shortly after he had arrived at the court from his native Seville. It is of note that, though the lively colours are very different from the earthen tones of his youthful work, due to his coming into contact with the rich collections of Venetian paintings owned by his master, Philip IV, one can still see the tenebrism of the early Baroque Period that would have him paint a scene in which, though an exterior, the lighting would still have an artificial quality to it.

DIEGO VELÁZQUEZ DE SILVA (1599-1660)

25 Vulcan's Forge (Cat. 1171)

Canvas (223 × 290 cm)
Spanish school. Baroque
17th century
Hall 15a

This mythological scene —of the adulterous affairs of the gods Venus and Mars— was composed by Velázquez during his first visit to Italy, where he went to study the Italian masters. This experience would change many aspects of earlier painting: he slowly drifted away from tenebrism, and he would also exchange his tight brush strokes for looser, softer ones. In this painting, he also incorporated the beauty of the nudes that he had studied in Italy: the bodies of the blacksmiths have a great classical feel. Of course, the scene is classical as well: the god Apollo descending to the depths of the earth where Vulcan, the divine blacksmith, laboured to inform him that his wife Venus, the goddess of love, was trysting with Mars, the god of war. The feeling of the moment, somehow quotidian, is one of Velázquez's achievements in this and other paintings.

24

25

DIEGO VELÁZQUEZ DE SILVA (1599-1660)

26 The Fable of Arachne, or The Tapestry-weavers (Cat.1173)

Canvas (220 × 289 cm)
Spanish school. Baroque
17th century
Hall 14

This Velázquez painting, considered for a long time to represent a generic theme, actually hides the depiction of a mythological theme draped in the every day labour of a tapestry workshop. It is the fable of Arachne, the spinner, who challenged the goddess Pallas Athena by weaving a tapestry of superior quality. Arachne was turned into a spider by the goddess of the arts —and war— who appears in the background robed in military dress. It is in the back of the workshop where the plot of the fable is carried out: in the foreground we see the actual labour of the workshop. Both spaces are graced with a magnificent and meticulous use of light and a freedom and looseness of brush strokes that make this painting one of the most valuable of those pre-dating Impressionism. This canvas was added on to in the 18th century, on the upper part and on both sides. It is not known if this was done to restore it to its original state (though it is thought that it may have suffered damages in the Alcazar fire of 1734) or if it was simply an attempt to complete the scene and render it larger.

26

DIEGO VELÁZQUEZ DE SILVA (1599-1660)

**27 The Family of Philip IV, or The Maids of Honour
«Las Meninas»** (Cat. 1174)
Canvas (318 × 276 cm)
Spanish school. Baroque
17th century
Hall 12

The word «meninos» (or the feminine «meninas») referred to the young court companions of the monarch's children. It is with this name that this famous painting was christened in the 19th century. Originally it was entitled «The Family» (of King Philip IV). The Infanta Margarita, the only living child and thus heiress to the throne, occupies the centre.

Velázquez appears to be expressing his faith in the continuity of that Spanish dynasty by including a self-portrait as he stands before a canvas on which he is painting a portrait of King Philip IV and Mariana of Austria, which can be seen reflected in the mirror in the background.

This painting is considered one of the greatest achievements of universal art; one of the reasons for this is its remarkable treatment of spatial perspective. Velázquez, like no other, knew how to capture atmosphere, the air itself in a sense, between figures and, above all, between the foreground and the background. In this way he was able to create the illusion of the space in his studio.

27

NICOLAS POUSSIN (1594-1665)

28   Parnassus (Cat. 2313)

Canvas (145 × 197 cm)
French school. Baroque
17th century
Hall 11

Parnassus was the sacred, mythological mount in Greece where Apollo
and the Muses lived. These nine daughters of Zeus watched over music,
poetry, the arts and sciences and they accompanied the god of beauty
and goodness, the young Apollo. Poussin renders them here surrounded
by poets and artists with laurel leaves they hope to present to Apollo;
the god offers a cup of nectar, the sacred libation of the gods, to one of
the figures who has been introduced by a Muse. The magnificent female
nude in the foreground represents the fountain of Castalia, the artesian
well bubbling up at the foot of Mount Parnassus, the water of which the
poets and artists used to purify themselves before entering the temple
of Apollo. This vision of a classical theme as painted by Poussin is, in
itself, an equally classical work. The French painter, who established
himself in Italy, is considered the best example of the Baroque classical
tendency. His admiration for the artists of the Renaissance and his in-
depth studies of antiquity produced a very serene, balanced style, with
lively, intense colouring, all of which enhanced his traditional spirit of
French classicism.

28

DOMENICOS THEOTOCOPOULOS,
«EL GRECO» (1540-1614)

29 The Nobleman with his Hand on his Chest (Cat. 809)

Canvas (81 × 66 cm)
Spanish school. Mannerism
16th century
Hall 10b

In a famous sonnet, the poet Manuel Machado began his description of this character with the following words: «This stranger is a Christian/of serious mien and black accoutrement, /where nothing glistens more than the hilt of his admirable Toledan quiddity...» Even when it was learned who this «stranger» was —Juan de Silva, the Notary Mayor of Toledo— the sketch has remained forever as an archetypical depiction of a Spanish nobleman: austere, spiritual and deeply serious. And this painting owes its great fame precisely to the paradigm of «the Spanish essence». The nobleman is dressed in black, with white embroidered collar and cuffs; only a thin golden chain —from which hangs a medallion— attempts to counter the blackness; the hilt of the sword is also gold.

All the expression of the subject is concentrated in that deep, abstract gaze, directed right at the viewer, with a clear evocation of those eastern images that El Greco must have painted in his youth in his native Greece.

29

DOMENICOS THEOTOCOPOULOS,
«EL GRECO» (1540-1614)

30 The Trinity (Cat. 824)

Canvas (300 × 179 cm)
Spanish school. Mannerism
16th century
Hall 9b

This large canvas was one of the first painted by El Greco after arriving in Toledo. It is the central painting in an altarpiece that he was commissioned to do for the church of a Toledan convent. In this powerful Trinity, the distortions and exaggerations that would come to characterise El Greco within the scope of his manneristic dematerialisation are not yet apparent. In this painting, one can see that his memories of Venice are still fresh (Venice controlled his native Crete at that time), as are the evocations of Michelangelo, which he had gleaned from a short visit to Rome. The rich colouring of the composition and meticulous anatomical treatment of Christ confirm this. The weight and force of Christ's body and the powerful legs of the angel on the left will later give way to the ethereal dematerialisation for which he would become so renowned.

DOMENICOS THEOTOCOPOULOS,
«EL GRECO» (1540-1614)

31 The Adoration of the Shepherds (Cat. 2988)

Canvas (329 × 180 cm)
Spanish school. Mannerism
17th century
Hall 9b

This painting was done thirty-five years after The Trinity. In it one can appreciate all the characteristic aspects of El Greco's late Mannerism: dematerialised figures, awkward positions, anatomical deformations, fervent religious passion, maximum spiritualisation, etc. While El Greco was at the end of his career as a Mannerist —this painting was done for his own funerary chapel— the artistic trends had for years been veering towards Baroque realism. And this scene can certainly be said to be totally beyond reality. There is not one detail that recognises space — neither the nativity scene nor the shepherd's gifts. It seems as if only the luminous spotlight on the Christ defines the surrounding bodies; even the angels appear to be flying as if their bodies had no weight.

30

31

T I Z I A N O   V E C E L L I O   D I   G R E G O R I O ,   « T I T I A N »

(circa 1490-1576)

32 Bacchanal (Cat. 418)

Canvas (175 × 193 cm)
Italian school. Renaissance
16th century
Hall 9

This painting by Titian was the counterpart of Garden of Loves, which hangs in the same hall. Both mythological themes were painted for the Duke of Ferrara and given to Philip IV as a gift by one of Titian's heirs, much to the consternation of Italian art experts. In this Bacchanal —or wine feast—Titian illustrates the mythological scene of the arrival of the god of wine to the Isle of Andros, dedicated to him because the rivers ran with wine instead of water. The isle's inhabitants await Bacchus' arrival —his ship with sails unfurled can be seen in the distance. The colouring and movement of the figures are magnificent; and, of course, note the splendid reclining female nude at whose side reels a handsome, albeit drunk, young man.

T I Z I A N O   V E C E L L I O   D I   G R E G O R I O ,   « T I T I A N »

(circa 1490-1576)

33 The Emperor Charles V at Mühlberg (Cat. 410)

Canvas (332 × 279 cm)
Italian school. Renaissance
16th century
Hall 9

Titian painted several portraits of the Emperor Charles V, who considered the artist his favorite painter and gave him his full confidence and friendship, not to mention an imperial noble title. The emperor chose his favorite painter to preserve for posterity the great victory of the empire over the Protestants at the celebrated Battle of Mühlberg. Titian depicted Charles V as the leader of the victorious army in a magnificent equestrian portrait that evokes the monuments of the great Roman emperors. The monarch is set against a beautiful wooded countryside, with a river —the battle occurred near the banks of the Elbe— and a late-afternoon light that suggests a kind of spiritual absorption. The vitality of the colours of the armour (currently at the Royal Palace's Armory), of the horse blanket and the helmet's plume contrast magnificently with the paleness and the certain melancholy on the face of the protagonist, who was then sick and soon to retire to Yuste (Cáceres).

32

33

JACOPO ROBUSTI, «TINTORETTO» (1518-1594)

34 Christ Washing the Disciples' Feet (Cat. 2824)

Canvas (210 × 533 cm)
Italian school. Renaissance
16th century
Hall 9a

This large canvas was painted by Tintoretto for the Church of St. Mark in Venice. It was acquired for the collection of Charles I of England and then bought by Philip IV at auction upon Charles' death. It dates from Tintoretto's youth, but is one of his finest works. The composition —in which the principal theme is seen off to one side, from the centre towards the right— is truly marvelous. The scene is developed on two planes, and in each of them, the figures and the objects and the geometric ground and architectural shapes serve to create a theatrical profundity that is quite spectacular. This profundity is accentuated even more by the treatment of the air —the aerial perspective— between the figures, which is «really» visible beneath the cloth. Equally surprising is the treatment of the light, its playful, foreshortened movement, and, above all, the study of the expressions of the protagonists.

PAOLO CALIARI, «VERONESE» (1528-1588)

35 Christ with the Doctors in the Temple (Cat. 491)

Canvas (236 × 430 cm)
Italian school. Renaissance
16th century
Hall 7a

The theme —wrapped by Veronese in an ambience worthy of a Venetian assembly— is inspired by the evangelical passage of St. Luke that relates the time spent by Jesus among the Hebrew religious elders and how they marvelled at his wisdom. Among those represented around Christ, dressed in luxurious, typically Venetian, garb, is a knight of the Order of the Holy Sepulchre (standing on the right) who may have been the one to commission the painting. Veronese organised the scene so that Christ would stand out from the others: the postures, gestures and the gazes are all directed towards the main protagonist. Even the architectural elements are organised in such a way as to make Jesus stand out: the two columns frame him, the stairway isolates and strengthens him, the curved line of the portico is directed at him and the colonnade in general creates a rich background. In the distance, in an empty central space reinforced by the diagonal line of the stairway, we can see Joseph and Mary returning to the temple in search of their son.

34

35

GUIDO DI PIETRO DA MUGELLO,
«FRA ANGELICO» (1387-1455)

36   The Annunciation (Cat. 15)

Wood (194 x 194 cm)
Italian school. Renaissance
15th century
Hall 4

The name Fra Angelico was given to the painter because of the great religious devotion that characterised his work, about which it was said that it seemed made by angels. He was a Dominican monk who lived at the beginning of the Renaissance in Florence. His style is very elegant, very devout and even mystic. His work, such as this one, is luminous and rich in colour, with figures of an idealised beauty. The Annunciation is the principal scene of this large upper panel, shared with the Banishment of Adam and Eve from the Garden of Paradise; this is why the temple occupied by the Virgin and the Archangel Gabriel appears to be in a natural setting. Below this double scene is a frieze of small tales relating the life of the Virgin, from the time of her Betrothal to the Assumption, including the Visitation, the Adoration of the Magi and the Purification at the Temple. The five paintings are all graced with small jewels.

36

SANDRO BOTTICELLI (1444-1510)

37 The Story of Nastagio degli Onesti (Cat. 2838, 2839 and 2840)

Panel I (83 x 138 cm)
Panel II (82 x 138 cm)
Panel III (84 x 138 cm)
Italian school. Renaissance
15th century
Hall 3

The three panels owned by the Prado Museum formed part of a series of four that Botticelli, the most important Italian «Quattrocento» painter, was commissioned to do on the occasion of the celebration of the marriage vows that would link two important Florentine families; and it seems that the four decorated the four panels of a «wedding ark». These three were donated to the Prado in 1940 by the Catalán politician Frances Cambó; the fourth is part of private collection in the United States. In them, Botticelli illustrated one of the stories told in Bocaccio's Decamerone. It is the nuptial story of the young Nastagio degli Onesti. Shunned by the woman of his heart, he was passing through a wood when he experienced a strange vision: that of a woman who was pursued and caught by a nobleman who tore her heart out and fed it to his dogs. Nastagio realised what this torment meant: it was the eternal punishment — recurring with a certain frequency — of a lady who spurned the love of a suitor who would commit suicide. The young man then arranged for a country outing in the same place where the tormenting vision had appeared to him and invited the proud maiden of his dreams. The scene repeated itself and the young woman, on Nastagio's urging to reconsider her position, agreed to marry him. The banquet scene of this wedding is the panel missing from the Prado.

37

R A F F A E L L O   S A N Z I O ,   « D E   U R B I N O »
(1483-1520)

38   The Holy Family of the Lamb (Cat. 296)

Wood (29 x 21 cm)
Italian school. Renaissance
16th century
Hall 2

Of all the Holy Families by Raphael the Prado is proud to own this small panel is by far the most exquisite. Besides dating from the painter's youth, it belongs to his Florentine Period, when he met Leonardo da Vinci and Michelangelo. Many influences can be noted from da Vinci in Raphael's early paintings: for example, the «sfumato», or gradual shading from one colour to another, with which the tenuous shadows that outline the face of the Virgin of the body of the Child are created. The meticulous, detailed background —including a scene of the Jews' flight from Egypt— also shows his precocious talent. Later on, when Raphael moved to Rome and earned renown as a great painter, he would give less and less importance to this kind of detail. The serenity of this work comes from the simple composition as well: the whole of the figures forms a kind of imaginary triangle of which Joseph's head would be the upper vertex. The painting is signed in the Virgin's cleavage: «Raffaello Urbinas MDVII» (Raphael of Urbino, 1507).

R A F F A E L L O   S A N Z I O ,   « D E   U R B I N O »
(1483-1520)

39   Christ Falls on the Way to Calvary, or «Il Spasimo di Sicilia» (Cat. 298)

Canvas (once wood) (318 × 229 cm)
Italian school. Renaissance
16th century
Hall 2

The title «Il Spasimo di Sicilia» by which this work is also known comes from the common name for the place where the artist was from, the Convent of St. Mary «dello Spasimo» in Palermo. In the royal collections, to which it was added during the reign of Philip IV, this painting was called «the most precious jewel in the world». It is the most meticulous of Raphael's paintings regarding its composition and the expressivenss of the figures. Regarding the compositional organisation of the painting, Raphael passes before us the lovers' path that, from from right to left, heads off into the distance on the left towards a tranquil, beautiful country scene. In the expressions of the figures themselves, we see how intensely they are living the tragedy in question, as well as those of the people who passively watch Christ fall.

38

39

LEONE LEONI (1509-1590) AND
POMPEO LEONI (1533-1608)

40   The Emperor Charles V Subduing Rage (Sc. 273)

Bronze (251 cm. in height)
Italian school. Renaissance
15th century
Hall 1

This bronze is one of the most beautiful pieces of Renaissance statuary. The two figures rise up over a plynth, around the circumferance of which is the inscription: «Caesaris virtute domitus furor» («Rage dominated by Caesar's valor»). On the same plynth, on the left, is another legend referring to the piece's creator. In Latin it reads: «Leone, the father, and Pompeo, the son, natives of Arezzo, made this. 1564.» It is probable that Leone actually made it and that his son only helped fire it. Celebrated in this sculptural group is a victory of the imperial troops; some argue that it is the conquest of Tunis, other the Battle of Mühlberg against the Protestants. In the statue of the emperor, the cloak is removable and the nude is worked in the fashion of the old deified Roman emperors. In his right hand he carries a lance that has felled the body of his vanquished foe, while in the left he has a sword, the hilt of which is shaped like an eagle's head.

40

MICHELANGELO MERISI, «CARAVAGGIO»
(1573-1610)

41 David Victorious over Goliath (Cat. 65)

Canvas (110 x 91 cm)
Italian school. Baroque
17th century
Hall 41

Michelangelo Merisi was known as Caravaggio because of his birthplace. He was a rebellious and independent artist who lived an adventurous, stormy life. His special interest for light and for faithfully representing reality allowed him to evolve a very personal, very realistic and tenebrist style. He is considered the father of this first trend in the Baroque Period, which won many followers among European painters in the first half of the 17th century. This painting, the only Caravaggio in the Prado, is an exact paradigm of these characteristics. The figures of the two protagonists —the young David and the Philistine giant Goliath— are set out in strong light on a background of shadows. The realism of the giant's severed head is certainly an example of dramatic naturalism. Also of note is the organisational composition, giving the scene ample space within the paradoxically tight dimensions.

GUIDO RENI (1575-1642)

42 Hippomenes and Atalanta (Cat. 3090)

Canvas (206 × 297 cm)
Italian school. Baroque
17th century
Hall 43

Guido Reni was one of the Baroque painters of the so-called Bologna school, responsible for a type of Baroque art that was different from the realist tenebrism of Caravaggio and his followers. The Classicists, as they were known, decided to do away with expressiveness and realist force and give more important to the richness of colour, a greater presence of light and, above all, to the cult of detailed, idealised beauty that would evoke the Renaissance and Raphael. Despite this, Guido Reni made some concessions to tenebrism in this magnificent work, noticeable in the effects of the light on the two marvelous nudes. These are the mythological characters of Hippomenes and Atalanta, who had an exciting footrace. The astuteness of Hippomenes —inspired by the goddess of love, since his prize for winning the race was Atalanta— was responsible for the golden apples falling to the ground and attracting Atalanta's attention. Distracted by such fine fruit, her suitor got the better of her.

41

42

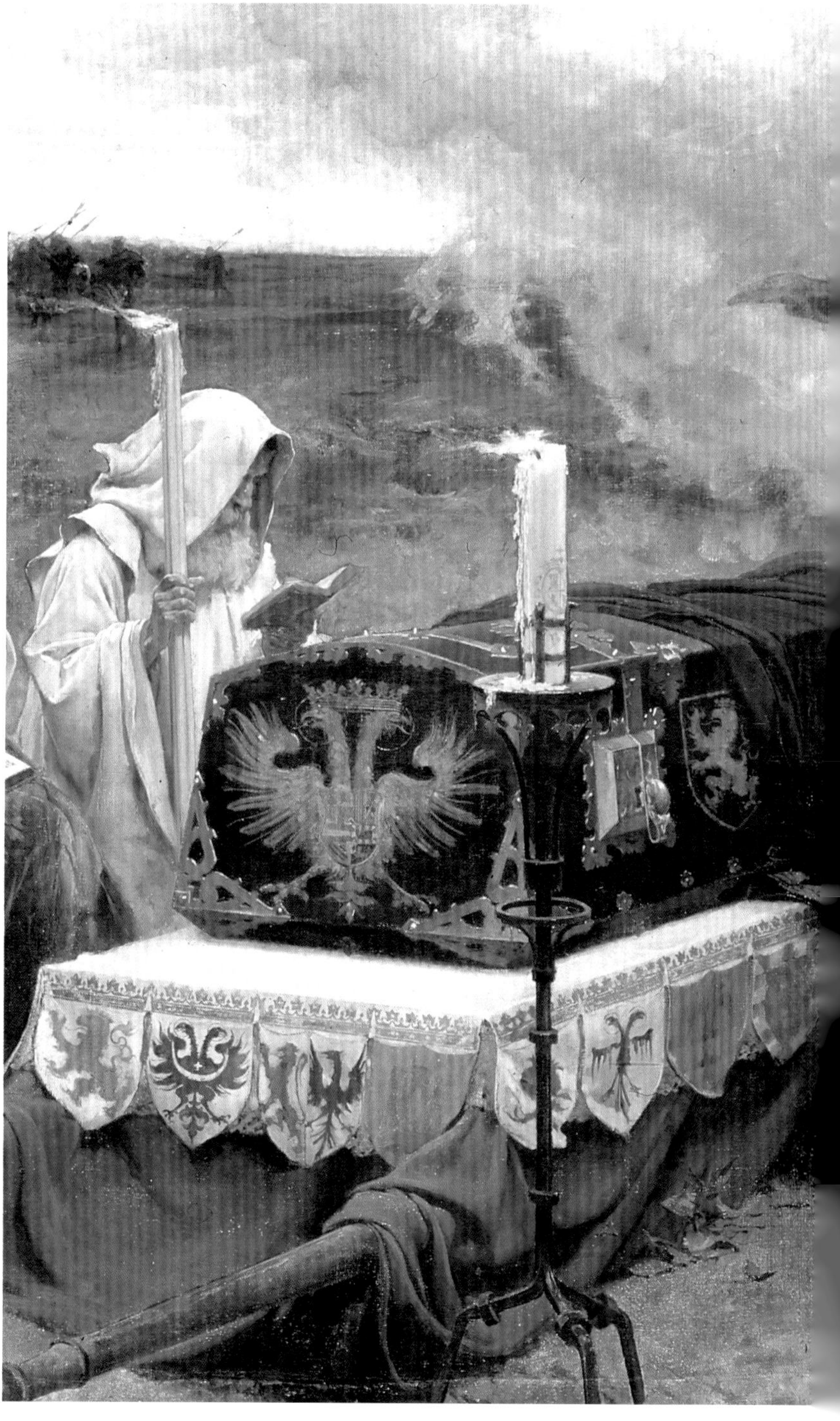

Francisco Pradilla Ortiz. Doña Juana la Loca (detail)

CASÓN DEL BUEN RETIRO

This building and the neighbouring Army Museum are the only architectural vestiges remaining of the Buen Retiro Palace, built for Philip IV in the 17th century. A sizeable part of the gardens that surrounded the palace is now the Buen Retiro Park.

At the Casón (which literally means «big house» but was coined for the building in the last century as a tongue-in-cheek allusion to its ruinous state), the Prado Museum exhibits its 19th and early 20th centuries painting collections, along with part of its sculpture collection from the same period.

The entrance is on Alfonso XII Street. The Masterpieces Tour continues in the halls to the right of the entrance.

JOSÉ DE MADRAZO AGUDO (1781-1859)

43 The Death of Viriato (Cat. 4469)

Canvas (307 × 462 cm)
Spanish school. Neo-Classical
19th century
Hall 2b

With this large canvas the interest in historical themes that was so characteristic of the 19th century began. In it, José de Madrazo evokes the death of Viriato, the famous guerilla leader who put up strong resistance to the Romans in the Iberia Peninsula in the second century B.C. The Romans finally bribed two of his soldiers to kill him while he slept. José de Madrazo presents the leader dead on his warrior's cot, surrounded by the sadness of some of his followers, the anger of others and the decision of the two stalking out of the tent to avenge the murder. Madrazo, who painted this canvas in Rome over a period of several years, left in it one of the finest examples of the neo-Classical Style and its most outstanding features: the importance of the drawing, common to the academic training of these artists; a certain carelessness regarding colour; and the practically sculptural air of the figures. The neo-Classical painters, hoping to resuscitate the aesthetic postulates of Greco-Roman antiquity, tended to be inspired —since there were no paintings from that time— by sculptures and classical ceramics, mostly linear and devoid of colour.

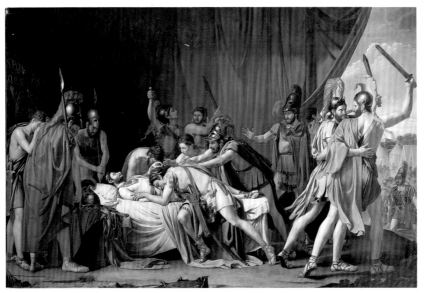

43

VICENTE LÓPEZ PORTAÑA

44 The Painter Francisco de Goya (Cat. 864)

Canvas (93 x 75 cm)
Spanish school. Neo-Classical
19th century
Hall 2

Vicente López succeeded Goya as the Royal Court Painter during the
reign of Ferdinand VII and did this portrait of the old master on the
occasion of a visit in 1826 to the court from the Aragonese elder, who
was by then living in Bordeaux.

Goya was then 80 and would die two years later. It is said that Goya got
bored with posing for his colleague, who was a stickler for detail, and
that for this reason the portrait is somewhat inferior to others by López.
However, for the very same reason, or perhaps because of the strong
personality of the model, this is one of López's most striking paintings.
Vicente López was a neo-Classical painter with certain traces of the
Rococco Style. In this impressive rendering of Goya's face, one can see
the neo-Classical emphasis on masterly drawing, though in this case it is
done with less rigidity, resulting in a remarkable depiction of the
features of the severe visage of the elderly Goya. With the warmer
shades of the palete and the back of the chair, he contrasts the cold
tones of Goya's suit. It would be difficult indeed to better reflect the
personality of the great Spanish painter Goya.

*The 19th century painting exhibition, arranged chronologically,
continues upstairs. The stairway is to be found at the exit of
the previous hall.*

44

FEDERICO DE MADRAZO Y KUNTZ (1815-1894)

45 Doña Amalia de Llano y Dotres, The Countess of Vilches (Cat.2878)

Canvas (126 x 89 cm)
Spanish school. Romanticism
19th century
Hall 7

Federico de Madrazo, father and son of painters, is the greatest figure in Spanish Romantic painting. He held high official posts —he was the Director of the Prado Museum on two occasions— and he was, and is, considered the finest portrait artist of this period, if not of the entire 19th century in the whole of Europe. He did over 500 private and court portraits (he was also Court Painter). In his work, exactness and tidiness took precedence over the psychological aspects of his subjects. In this work, he presents the Countess of Vilches, Doña Amalia de Llano y Dotres, a member of Madrid's high-society who married the Count of Vilches. She was a cultured woman who would write and publish several forgettable novels. In the portrait she is elegantly dressed, reclining on a large chair and rendered with an extremely delicate and deliciously romantic air. The meticulous detail of her face and arms reveal Madrazo's interest in drawing —which he learned from his father at the Fine Arts Academy—and the reason that the Romantic trend he represented was referred to as «purist».

MARIANO FORTUNY MARSAL (1838-1874)

46 The Painter's Children in the Japanese Hall (Cat. 2931)

Canvas (44 x 93 cm)
Spanish school. Realism
19th century
Hall 11

This painting is without a doubt a small jewel. Though because of its size it might be considered a minor work, it is actually one of Fortuny's most brilliant. The painter, the first Spaniard to become a truly cosmopolitan artist, enjoyed international fame and earned a large number of commissions throughout his short life. However, in this little piece —Fortuny was certainly a specialist in small formats— he was not concerned with a commission. He painted it just a few months before he died, never really finishing it; it is a reflection of his search in the last years of his life to find new roads and outlets for his painting. Thus, while some elements of the scene —such as the girl's leg— are perfectly drawn with meticulous detail, other parts of the paintings show such loose, separated brush strokes that one might say this presages Impressionism. The children in the painting are Mariano and María Luisa, the product of his marriage to Cecilia Madrazo, the daughter of Federico Madrazo.

45

46

JOAQUÍN SOROLLA Y BASTIDA (1863-1923)

47 Children at the Beach (Cat. 4648)

Canvas (118 × 185 cm)
Spanish school. Luminism (Impressionism)
19th century
Hall 13

Luminism is a term describing the contribution to Impressionism made by
Sorolla and other Mediterranean painters. To the knowledge and influences
that Sorolla had gleaned in Paris from the second generation of
Impressionists —the so-called post-Impressionists— he was able to add his
special interest in the dazzling light of the beaches along his native
southeastern Spanish coastline and his enthusiasm for colour. It can be said
that light and colour are the two great protagonists of this facet of Joaquín
Sorolla. In this particular case, as in others of beach scenes, the explosion of
light is blended with the capricious fervor of the water. The presence of
children helps to accentuate even more the joy of the scene. This painting
was signed and dated in 1910, and Sorolla kept it for a long time, exhibiting
it in private shows of his work in various cities in the United States. He later
donated it to Spain's Museum of Modern Art, whose 19th century collection
moved to the Prado when the former museum was closed.

*The exhibition continues on the lower floor; go down the stairs to enter,
on the right, the Grand Central Hall.*

47

EDUARDO ROSALES GALLINA (1836-1873)

48 **Queen Isabella's Will** (Cat. 4625)

Canvas (290 × 400 cm)
Spanish school. Realism
19th century
Hall 1a (or Large Hall)

This painting afforded Eduardo Rosales, whose many problems and illnesses made his artistic life less than perfect, definitive renown: and it was only at the end of his life that his worth was truly appreciated. This painting earned him first prize —and the sale of the canvas to the State— at the National Exposition of 1864. He also presented it at the Paris International Exposition, where it it earned him a First Medal and the title of Knight of the Legion of Honour. When Rosales was searching for a theme for his entry at the National Exposition he wanted «to find a matter of great importance in our history», which turned out to be the will that Isabella left upon her death, considered the finest such document of its kind and an exposé of her political philosophy. Isabella appears on her deathbed, with canopy and curtains, dictating to her seated scribe the contents of the will. Sitting in a chair, bent and spent, is King Ferdinand, with their daughter and heiress, Princess Juana, known as «La Loca». In the group on the right is the covered figure of Cardinal Cisneros, who would later become Regent of Castile.

FRANCISCO PRADILLA ORTIZ (1848-1921)

49 **Doña Juana la Loca** (Cat. 4584)

Canvas (340 × 500 cm)
Spanish school. Realism
19th century
Hall 1a (or Large Hall)

Francisco Pradilla did several effigies of Juana la Loca, and there are several in the Prado; many other 19th-century painters did the same. Within the historical trend of this century's painting, the insane Castilian princess was a common model. This painting won a Medal of Honour, its first, at the 1878 National Exposition. It captures a moment when the princess' entourage take a break during the long march she undertook to transfer the body of deceased husband, the Archduke Philip «the Handsome». Her insanity, accentuated over a long period by jealousy, moved her to undertake this trip (from Burgos to Granada, where she wished to bury her husband), only traveling at night because «an honest woman should flee from the light of day when she has lost her husband, who was the sun.» During the day, the casket was kept at monasteries along the way, though in this painting we see a convent of nuns and not a monastery of monks as should have been the case: Juana wanted to get the casket out of this church though, because she was jealous of any female eye being set upon her dearly departed husband.

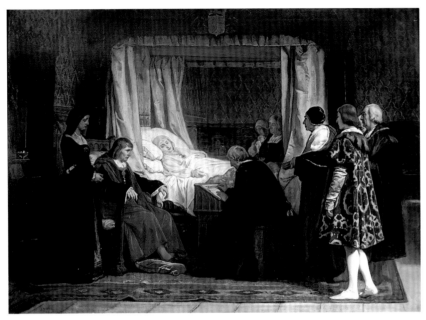

48

49

JUAN GRIS (JOSÉ VICTORIANO GONZÁLEZ)
(1887-1927)

50 Portrait of Josette (Cat. 4389)

Wood (116 x 63 cm)
Spanish school. Cubism
20th century
Hall 3b

The 20th-century paintings belonging to the Prado Museum are currently displayed at the Renia Sofía National Art Centre. The collection includes donations and contemporary legacies by Picasso (Guernica, among others), Miró and Juan Gris. Of the collection, only this painting by Gris has remained at the Prado. It was donated by the collector Douglas Cooper, who specified that it be the property of the Prado Museum and not of the Spanish State. Juan Gris, born and educated in Madrid, moved to Paris before he was twenty, where artists from all over the world were experimenting with avant-garde trends and styles. There he met Picasso and the French painter Braque, along with those who would become the leading figures of Cubism. This style is visible in the portrait of his companion Josette; as a Cubist painting, the work contains the decomposed reality of multiple geometric elements, an approach designed to present the most significant aspects of the images. In the grayish whole, we can distinguish the figurative elements: head, hands and a stool.

50

© ALDEASA® : 1994

Depósito Legal: M-2482-1994

ISBN: 84-8003-022-4

Design and Layout: Mar Lissón / Natàlia Arranz

General Coordination: Ángeles Martín / Paula Casado

Translation: SAT

Photographs: Museo del Prado / Oronoz

Photocomposition: Grafitex S.A., Barcelona

Photomechanical Production: Gamacolor, Madrid

Printed in Spain by: TF, Madrid

(Printed in Spain)